DEDICATION

This book talk about Human Thinking Functions and has shown four of functions. To know the Person, just to improve some precision, many problems can be solved, many disasters can be avoided.

We can be sure that when science use on society, there is the Real Social Science or the "Social Science" has the required scientific contents, the progress of human society can be speeded up, and the progress of human beings can use with peaceful manner.

Thank you !

Fanzhu meng

Chicago.

CONTENTS

ACKNOWLEDGMENTS

Thank you every reader, my readers will understand my contribution.

Thank you Createspace.com, the self-publishing system.

Chapter 1

Overview

Section 1　Logic and Science

At first, the human brain has Logic Function, and then, man has put it into use.

The ultimate principles of application of Logical Function (Logic Function) are very simple, as wise men who had summarized of formal logic: the law of identity, the law of contradiction, etc. About the laws how to express it is another matter, truly to use the Logical Rule or Logical Function---Human beings seemingly need not the training.

To everyone, the Logical Function is equipped by physiological function, and the rules of application which are using are spontaneous. Human being uses

Logical Function to solve a problem, the true difficulty does not on the Logical Rules, usually is that such as application conditions of Logical Function.

The word "science" had generated ago, the Logic Function of Human Thinking Function which has already been existing. The word or this type of words had generated about hundreds of years later, the applications of Logical Function had achieved a large scale, the applications had solved the issues so lots.

People classified science into some kind, the methods were according to the object or the objective issues which were solved, later, a various category of science took shape successively. Yes, people have the generic sorting technique which are by consequence by "object" for dividing gist. Also seemingly take the thorough, serious method,---it is usually called as science or scientific method.

"Science", the word had generated in the front, the systematic scientific knowledge in the back. So, the word is in the front, it delineated the matter following its back.---This is a very antic relationship, but the fact exactly is.

This kind of matters are lots, some of them are creating that fatal problems or unnecessary discussions. For example, the "nation".

For hundreds of years, science (scientific method) have analyzed, have processed lots of matters. This moment the pseudoscience swarm out, nearly anyone what took "solemn parlance" it can be crown with "science", but, they usually are of the rhetoric technology good, that is scientific parlance, almost no scientificity any more.

The scientific parlance is irreproachable, but, when the scientific parlance can cover up whose relating in pseudoscience it is a big problem. Generally speaking, a pseudoscience looks like a science then keeps a foothold, it needs a scientific parlance at least.

"Science", it essential meanings are that face on "known", then use Logical Function (Logic Function), apply Logical Rules.

Firstly make sure the application conditions of Logical Function and Logical Rules, which must be near arrived "known" enough. When cannot reach on "known", although use the Logical Function or

Logical Rule, it cannot get the logical consequence.

The Logical Function, the Logical Rule which can be used on anywhere almost, these days, the gross of logical knowledge is immense already. Every one of each classified scientific knowledge, in fact, is the consequence of Logical Function apply. And, each category of scientific knowledge, all of them must be has the feature which can meet logical rules.

Any matter, any issue, when it truly achieve "known", therefore, can use Logical Rules, can scientifically dispose of them. This common phenomenon is that science be introduced into a matter, a new field, hereafter, precisely observe them if it obtained gross of achievements enough, would be called a "category" or a "discipline" of science.

Now, to bake bread, for example, only adjust the rotary knob, it is all of the thing work out. Because you knew key index: temperature and time. In history, to bake bread, need so long time for gather experience, one need learn light a fire may beginning one's childhood.---This is a scientific approach and technological achievements, integrated "science" introduced into a specific matter.

People who talk about "generalize scientific approach", frequently is including contents two:

1. Generalize scientific approach.

2. Be used else scientific achievements.

But, a simple scientific approach which in generalizing is a simple thing:

1. Make the matter into a "known" degree.

2. Use Logic Function, use Logical Rules.

3. Build logical consequence(s).

With scientific approach introduce into a matter or a new field, if can combine else scientific achievements to solve the practical problems, it so complex, however, it is good, it is a successful popularizer of the scientific approach.

Section 2 Real Social Science

Any kind of science, it necessarily has scientific

nature and can be described, it has correlative logical chains inside, and each logical chain has a specific logical starting point, and every one of conclusion with adequate cause and/or necessary cause.

In that way, now, think over again: frequently called of social science which whether has scientificity or not, and how to describe?

Unfortunately, the answer can prove that so-called of social science is not belong to a science.

Real social science, it must have the scientificity which can be described.

When the field of traditional social science be introduced of the scientific method and then has the scientificity, hereafter, it precisely is a genuine social science.

This moment, in the special period of argument, for to distinguish the traditional statement, tentatively calls the name of this book talk about is "Real Social Science".

If: this "social science" or a discipline, its main

researching contents can be solved on this level:

1. Be analyzed to be "known".

2. Can use with sufficient reason, necessary reason.

3. Can to build the logical conclusions.

The scientificity of social science is established, real social science is established.

Real Social Science, concerns else mankind's science, concerns human beings how to cross the obstacle of different times timely safely, it according to scientific way and it pledge human beings can go further. So, this is a most important science, maybe is ultimate science.

Section 3   An Important Fact

Why human being can produce such as buildings, ships, planes and so on, produced such magnificent achievements?

At present, can trace back to the primary cause is

that because mankind has the unique Human Thinking Function.

Human Thinking Function, it seems that is a natural phenomenon, is a true, is a fact, however, is a kind of existence.

This kind of existence is very important, it leads to human being surpass to all of biology have known.

These days, the existence, the fact is still in mysterious or in unclear. To uncover this fact which contributes to more accurately, scientifically answer such topics of "everything for people", and contribute to mankind to build a nice Social Order.

So far, medical science or anatomy which cannot point out why human brain can produce the logical ability, else creatures, although have a brain which haven't Logical Function, which cannot calculate a simple calculation.

In the final analysis, the human brain has lots functions, all are else creatures too far behind to catch up with, therefore, mankind has complicated groups, precise cooperation, therefore, has high buildings and large mansions, automobiles, aircrafts, so on and so forth.

Can use the inverse method to deduce the function of the human brain from the consequence of brain did. It probably can be divided into ten more items, but, this book only shows four items which are of great importance:

1. Faith Function, this thinking function can set up hypotheses or imaginings such effect, and this function has the feature is that firstly believe without argument. This function particularly has significant value for the human being to exploit knowledge, it often stands on starting status of knowledge. In addition, this function lead everyone to think about where is mankind from? Where is the human going? Such Ultimate Questions.

2. Logic Function, it uses known to deduce unknown for new known. This function has important value for the human being to build knowledge systems, which can be used repeatedly.

3. The Sense of Mission Function, is that act on human future, human entirety. This function lead human being has been generated of future consciousness and group consciousness. Its

powerful and influential feature is a sense of responsibility, which lead man can undertaker for something.

4. Conscience Function, as far as possible do not damage else.

How did? Who did? And why is such complex Human Thinking Function? Obviously, these are big questions, these questions are Ultimate Questions, the answer will involve Ultimate Truth, Ultimate Fact.

People cannot avoid this kind of questions even no answer.

Human beings are fighting each other, are arguing each other, even various trouble, all they directly relate the situation, such Ultimate Questions, no answer.

There is no answer too, only provide a safe thinking to think.

The topic is following the fashionable statement, the theory of evolution. Firstly, approximately to show the theory of evolution:

1. Species are all come from evolving, and still in among of evolving.

2. The principle of evolution is that survival of the fittest. To physiological function be using be developing, be abandoning be abolishing, etc.

The theory of evolution nearly is correct, and people have been known clearly, even knew how to take advantage of the principle of the theory of evolution to filtrate zoology, botany for wanted.

What is said of the safety program, it is that hope people end of the idea of "naturally, randomly", because the idea leads to person's behavior randomly.

Evolving, had been happening, have been happened sequentially, was (are) a truth. But, only is a part of the truth. Should take notice of: except theory of evolution which said, have else principles which can be proved.(easily). The principles:

1. Had (has) been built the main function which was (is) invariability always. (The main function of the advanced creature was put into the brain for each one.)

2. Else, allowed can change what in a range. (So,

the theory of evolution can keep a foothold, which had used of reason was this reason.)

Over here "had been built" or "was put" so on, obviously indicate the invisible "Creator".

Now, discuss if have "Creator" by evidence which in Human Thinking Functions.

The Sense of Mission Function, the Faith Function or Logic Function, by one or all of them, to consider, must discover that, so far, man cannot to work out a theoretic route for to build such functions. These days, the anatomy cannot explain why is human brain can produce such thinking functions. About human brain how can produce such Human Thinking Functions, so far, really have a few discoveries, but to accurate cognition have a long way. Although the four items of thinking functions which seemingly clearly go on outward manifestation, the human brain has a working mechanism which is complex, mystery indeed. People cannot sure the brain cell how to produce the Sense of Mission Function, the integral consciousness, and future consciousness such working principle. Cannot point out where has been produced of Faith Function by physiologic construction, what working principle could lead man to think primal questions, ultimate questions. And, cannot explain that why all are brain cell are working, only human brain cell produced Logical Function which produced inferential capability.

Like that, only according to evidence which has shown of objective action, using the "known" make a theoretic deductive conclusion. The conclusion is conservative, reliable but is in negativity:

1. Human brain's functions, Human Thinking Functions, not by nature generated naturally, and, is not random generation.

2. These functions are not induced by an external condition, and are not caused by survival pressure.

For example, the Faith Function which impact the scope great than individual life scope, if said the function can be produced from survival pressure be entirely groundless, if said the function can be produced from personal experience that is entirely groundless too.

Instance by the Sense of Mission Function is more obvious. This function is the main working on that lead person who to undertake something. To everybody, obviously is that this function made the survival risks increase more.

Tentative judgment is that, however, the human brain, Human Thinking Functions had been formed, so, the human is a purposive precision creature and, was from some kinds of beforehand design.---This design, this design's intention, to this day's human knowledge is so inconceivable.

There, have been touching of the Ultimate Question, Ultimate Truth. To do this, anyone hasn't to talk these by nonsense, hasn't to affirm something randomly. Only have to pay attention on the truth. However, the fact has already been happened, happening, the truth, the fact, as sure as fate, the miracle which has been existing.

Above, wanted to suggest to people that have a outlook on life or outlook on world, do not affirm the theism, the atheism or "theory of science" which one is correct prematurely, for human society can step forward continually, and in a peaceful manner, should know the specific aim is that rediscovering, rethinking.

Above, isn't that the theism is correct enough, only is that the theism is more accurate, more reliable, but, this theism is different than before.

Human Thinking Function, maybe is a coincidence from Nature, maybe Creator had, has built deliberately, (Even the process is not over.), even also reason do not take into account, three caused or more, all ok. But, all sorts of views:

1. Should to mutual respect.

2. Have to query each other. (Do not refuse, this is a necessary procedure.)

However, each side, all kinds of opinion has to, have to cherish this one:

This kind of fact, is hard-won, only one.

Acknowledge the Human Thinking Function, admit this fact, can give rise to lots religions, political parties or similar institutions to think deeply with objective, evenhanded thinking. But, Almost no, the reason is:

About the Sense of Mission Function is real existing to someone, but, about the theory of faith, may only is a name. Someone is involuntarily to take Power to control social order for oneself dignity, and all kinds of material benefit. Someone refuses these kinds of thinking with fear.

Human Thinking Function, can be described in any way, even try to describe more details. But, in any case, need to esteem this important fact, base on this fact:

1. For theistic religion, "Creator" or "God" had been, has been created everything, the highest creature, summit product is the human being, any religious doctrine or any religious activity should to protect the highest product, should not try to tamper the highest creature. Do not to damage the Human Thinking Function. Or else, is not theism.

2. For "scientific socialism" or political parties, human society is exactly base on human attributes, base on Human Thinking Function.---Hereunder, can think human future. The

Human Thinking Function is fact, if not believe in God or Creator, must admit the fact, believe in Nature. But, more clear is that because Nature made lots of impossible coincidences have caused the Human Thinking Function. Therefore, any social scientific theory, any social science, any social practice, must esteem this natural miracle, protect the Human Thinking Function. Or else, is pseudoscience.

Any topic which core content includes human core content must base on Human Thinking Function, this is a simplest, the most basic principle.

For facts, are that no this fact, no anything.

(If) the lack of precision in recognizing this fact, must be that leads to numerous errors in behavior. In fact, many efforts are meaningless because this fact is ignored.

Human four thinking functions are a parameter of social science. This is a lowest standard index (indicator). If reduce this precision of index, this parameter haven't calculating significance.

Section 4 Function---System---Society

The functional theory isn't a new invention. There, in the case, dividing different function to expose each system, it explains that because each function is in different cause and can classified every difference,---even it lead the descriptive approach is of difference.

Faith Function Knowledge System, the Sense of Mission Function Knowledge System, Selfish Desire knowledge System, etc, all be due to a certain function generated, and a system, each knowledge system has own generic type, each one has own direction. When they be mixed of the debates is almost insignificance.

There, try to divide them and, only is dividing of three to show three systems, there for a proof: Function, true enough is in existence, and the functions give rise to the classification which is objective.

Even though only two knowledge systems have

been mixed then argue, there are no right or no wrong. If one want to talk reality, another one wants to talk future, two people else indefinitely, randomly change, the argument could be exactly chaining of each mouth.

What is more, if two kinds of knowledge got mixed and occupy a person's mind, cannot be distinguished clearly, would give rise to the person's mind which could be two functions enter into a tangle.

As to Power, why have been generated the dictatorial Power, the Enjoying Type Power? And that the dictators are almost each one nearly has praiseworthy the Sense of Mission Function, to their situations of Selfish Desire Function, someone is almost zero, may someone is extreme dilate. The reason about this, the Power is dysfunction, then, the Power has been accepted of the dictator of dysfunction.

This book says the Power, has two meaning, one is a natural attribute, another one is a man-made which functions is lowered, is reduced.

Inspect the Functions, contribute to discern Functions which made the consequences.

About knowledge system, if compare the Logical Knowledge System with the Hypothesis Knowledge System (Faith Function knowledge System), will be knowing it why is different, because is that two knowledge system come from two Functions. To differentiate the two kinds of system, for example, it contribute to the two type, each one safely continuing until can be scientized, however, right now, cannot.

Talk about Human Thinking Function, to anyone, all is that: a person is a system, which due to the main function guide out. Each person can repair and improve their own Thinking Functions to make their serial behaviors more meaningful.

The aggregate effect of various Functions will produce comprehensive consequences, so the theory of "Social Functions" is also true.

Held by system theory, this book is based on the abstract understanding, mainly in order to solve the major issues, it can also help people obtain the objective survey, objective viewpoint about each self, each one.---This is very important, because of the relentless thought and serious criticism need most people can have been held a calm, objective attitude.

To see any person as a system, it is not only a view, a fair transcendental view, but also points out a fact, it also good for people when observing anyone, including self can be on facts, then can be based on the facts to solve the actual problems.

Man is a system, is a developed out from man's Thinking Function, the main function.

This book only is a beginning, cannot talk about man's main function in more detail and, cannot point out any functional reason. But, has already been affirmed: any behavior must belong to a system.

Specific behavior, series behaviors, a behavior system, once have a problem, the main function must have a problem in advance, firstly.

It is an objective issue to examine behavior system whether has a problem or not, first thing is that to check system's main function.

Social activities or a Power is that too, to examine their main function, to survey behavior system, that all is an objective issue.

The whole of society is a big system. How are the

system or how are its subsystem, if there are any unnecessary redundant or absent or dysfunction, the big system or subsystems are in abnormality, these are all is that face on objective facts.

As for the person, everyone: we all need to constantly examine our main function, our system.

As to society, it is a system which is consisting of several subsystems:

1. Unit of Social Activity.

2. Knowledge system.

3. Order–Procedure.

Among which:

1. Unit of Social Activity: 1.) Man. 2.) The combinations of man (men) and equipment(s). 3) The combinations of people.

2. Knowledge system: 1.) The Logic Function Knowledge System. 2.) Faith Function Knowledge System 3.) The Sense of Mission Function Knowledge System. 4.) Selfish Desire Function Knowledge System, etc.

3. Order-Procedure. 1.) Artificial part. 2.) Preset part.

Obviously, above only displays this book think to be the important parts.

What is the relationship between each system?

Within the large system of human society, the person, this system situation of functions will have an impact on the knowledge systems, on other Units of Social Activity, etc. And the consequences of that impact will be reflected back to each person.

The systems interact with each other. Therefore, to do that be beneficial to human society:

1. If you start with any system, you can get a substantial benefit.

2. Starting from all the systems, and of course, you can get a substantial benefit.

3. starting from the critical system, can get the most significant benefit.

4. The Human Thinking Function is the key to the critical system.

Human society is a system. So, the main function of the system is complicated, to it can be trying on a simplified.---Person's thinking functions to be the core of the system's functions, the border is the preset Order-Procedure. At this point, the main function of the Power or any Unit of Social Activity, all of they are only a periodic consequences.

The two key parts of the human society were, are, will in preset. Human being(s) the activities space is always between both ends. That human destiny is (be) predetermined.

To quest for destiny or the future which is always been a fascinating task to individual or humanity. It's not possible to accurately predict the fate of human beings. It's probably worth to take a rough assessment.

With the above function(s) which have been describing, as to the Human beings, the first and most important conclusion is that:

The human being is great, and second is great too, after any disaster, humans still great.---This is guaranteed by the Creator or Nature.

Like that, these days, what is the necessity to study social science?

No, only is that:

1. It is that Human Thinking Function has been specified, man (humans) necessarily to do that in any way.

2. It is the Order-Procedure has been stated. Would say that not to study today or not to study tomorrow, but sooner or later must be.

What's the difference between early research and late research?

No big difference.

Thousands of years of early or late study, to human history long, it is same only a few seconds of errors.

The number of tens of billions of people continue to be stupid and obsessed by a stupidity, these are in contrast to the total number of people in human history, not more than parts per billion.

If another billion people be killed again by the wrong knowledge systems and the wrong Units of Social Activity or a Power as had happened, the total number, not more than parts per billion in human history.

So, anyone, any political party, any religious

organization or any others groups they can try detached thinking to think like this: the purpose of Social Science, only is this meaning to walk on the right track as soon as possible, as soon as possible to end of hoax, avoid to kill one billion people again,--- That's all.

With such objective thoughts, it is not difficult to find systemic problems, to find our own systems, to others systems, if have some problems, to find solutions easily.

Because, human beings have the Human Thinking Functions, and the Order-Procedure, which was, is, will always guarantee human value.---Human beings will never die.

Chapter 2

The Person

Section 1 Concept --Standard --Index

To give a definition for answers the question--- What is the person?---Could be known that this question is always difficult.---Human beings know themselves, each individual knows himself, the "know(s)" is a process which can never end of continue.

Now, redefining of the Person which is just increased a precision.

The new definition which includes traditional physiological indexes, and then add the Human Thinking Functions.---Human being (be) is this creature having the Human Thinking Functions.

In fact, people's thinking function is also an indicator of physiology. A usual individual has this index (indicator), and then there is the actual content of the indicator which has the actual representation and display.

With four thinking functions as indexes, the following contents are not only four thinking functions but also indicators are that must be displayed as well:

1. Healthy and sane thinking functions. (In this case, only four terms are included)

2. Knowledge of a certain scale. (Average level of the era)

3. Have a certain degree of willpower and ability of self-control. (General criteria for adapting to the environment of society and achieving oneself)

The latter two can be understood as follows: The fish, which has the function of swimming in the water and, can actually swim in water. The eagle, which has the function of flying and, can actually fly.

The owner of thinking functions must have a

certain scale of knowledge, and the process of accumulating knowledge will naturally produce willpower and ability of self-control.

The above indicators, whether are (is) equipped in fact, the situation has the value of "known", is the basis for the simple inference as this:

1. One's character or morals of the average can be inferred.

2. We can deduce the criminal probe data of the society or an individual by a new manner.

3. Individual life expectancy of the average can be inferred.

4. The quality of the state or the society or a person can be inferred.

With the concept and indicators of human, it can be described in a scientific and digital way---"Human Content", "Person content", "Human Purity", etc.

"Human purity",(Person content), (Human Content), a cruel phrase, it suffers a moral questions of the problem easily. Give an answer, of course, it is to avoid the possibility of misunderstanding: the phrase easily to define of the Person so scientific digitalization, and then the definition does not contradict the thinking of the conscience, and this definition provides a scientific base for moral rescue or relief for someone.

"Human Content", could be like such phrases "Gold content", "Water content" and so on, it is more suitable for answer quantitative contents, it is explaining of purity.

The "Human Content" is different than such as "gold content" that Human Thinking Function which is in physiologic possession, it is easy to be changed if implemented to specific individuals.

The digitalised consideration, it is more appropriate to answer the following questions:

1. Whether the (each) individual basically conforms to the basic design, basic intention of the Creator or Nature.

2. Everyone be easier to examine own thinking functions. It is more convenient to pursue the perfection of "Human Content".

3. Finally, and most importantly, any theory or system do not attempt to reduce "Human

Content" or, in fact result in such reductions.

Trying to look at human beings from the universe, and then, look at human beings again could be more objective. Mankind may be made in Creator maybe made in Nature, however, it is that:

Man is the greatest work.

With the Human Thinking Function, human's action to all things is of vital importance. In order to put an end to the controversy about whether the mankind is noble creature or not, (even the answer is not in reality), to avoid devaluing human beings on philosophical, theological or scientific, there, it's so clearly say that even do not care where people come from, who had, have made human beings, however, mankind is the highest work of the Creator or Nature, or man is the most amazing coincidence of nature. One of the important ways in which Creator or Nature arranges the universe is the man.

Man is a system, is the most basic system.

The human social system is developed by the most basic system. Human Thinking Function to everyone is the main function, and made each one is an individual system. It is an amazing system that can develop knowledge, store knowledge, and master complex knowledge.

This system to constitute other systems, a knowledge system, an organizational system, even the entire human society system, etc, it is conclusive important, there are all made by human.

Every person, each of us is a system. It is not creating a new idea, it is not making up a new story, is a scientific view that's true:

1. The situation of everyone is first the cause, the main function has made of the situation, the main function determines the system.

2. Review the main function and the whole system. It is easy to get detailed information about each one.

3. The main function if be in normal, the system be in normal too, and vice versa.

This basic system is of decisive importance to other systems and to the entire human social system:

1. The quality of this system generally affect the quality of other systems.

2. The reaction of other systems if also determined of every system, the first change be from this system.

As a scientific research, the concept and index of mankind which is the base for analyzing social reality even to plan a social order:

1. The usual situation of the individual(s) affect the quality of society generally.

2. The usual situation of the individual(s) generally affect the social order.

3. The general situation of the individual(s) generally affect the quality of other Units of Social Activity.

4. The general situation of the individual(s) generally affect the quality of Power (man-made).

The concept and index of the Person can be used to deduce national conditions:

1. The human situation, the basic system situation importantly affect the situation of other

systems in the country and the overall system of the country.

2. The human situation is a basis and is a systematic condition, which affect the vitality, creativity of a country and determines country's competitiveness.

The concept and the index of the human being(s), which become a new supplement---A variety of topics which bases on people-centered should know the concept, indexes:

1. Such as Freedom---to think about a healthy, sane thinking function firstly, the freedom is more clearly.

2. Such as Human rights---to think about a healthy, sane thinking function firstly, the human rights are becoming a nobler.

3. Such as Demography, (or Malthusism), ballot ticket.etc. Should to know what is the basic reason.

Section 2 Responsibilities and Obligations

(Application)

First of all, everybody has (automatically) the obligation and responsibility to meet the concept which in have been said, and, achieve the standards of the indicators, (indexes), that have the following meanings:

1. The basic intention of the Creator or Nature to design human beings which should be realized.

2. In other systems, in the overall large system, the person is a positive system with practical value.

3. You are really living, lived as a high "Human Purity".

Everyone should to think comprehensively on responsibilities for oneself, for society, for the Creator, or for Nature. Therefore, self-improvement is a lifelong pursuit.

Second, other people, other Units of Social Activity, other systems, have the same responsibilities and obligations to each individual:

1. Respect the highest work of the Creator or

Nature. Treasure every life. Praise every perfect system.

2. Do not destroy any one, do not attempt to tamper the highest work of the Creator or Nature.

3. Do not undermine the Human Thinking Functions, the critical basic social system.

Section 3   Objective Treatment (Application)

It is a kind of transcendence and virtue to everyone to examine own main function, to survey own system timely and often.

Most people check their car before an important trip, it is a good habit. Now using this instance to tell people that, it is similar to the example, and more important, to constantly examine your own thinking function, to examine your own system.

The first several times may not be used to, or even don't know what to detect. Later, the habit becomes familiar and more effective. At the very least, there should test seriously before a major events. It is responsible to yourself and to society.

Value of Autognosis:

If all of thinking functions or one have (has) become a defect or a variation, which is (be) always limit or/and disorder the main functions.---This is a theorem.

Based on the four thinking functions to talk, any one of them when limited, which must reflect the behavior's system accordingly. Anyone of them if changed, the corresponding behavior's system will be in behavioral malformation. If the four thinking functions be chaotic, the behavior's system inevitably is be in chaos.

The four thinking functions play an important role in the studying or a judgment of macro issues, if one or all of them be (are) changed into a malformation, who will cant to analyze religious, political such issues with clear thinking.

How does to analyze own four thinking functions? In the beginning can try to check one of them with simple things, and then try to deepen and wide range. Below show two examples:

1. About the Faith Function, look at the Faith Function's products that you are using, and look at the society if also have others.

2. About the Sense of Mission Function, look at what you're using of products, and to check what you are doing trust in, also to check what are used in the society. Own Sense of Mission Function, whether still has, still is multilevel, still is a multi-directional function. If one has been limited, what are the types? Examine what you are considering which to be your so-called obligations.

If you find that the functions are limited, you should pay attention to that your own system got an illness, and your behaviors have been limited on some kinds, and you can also find the restricting type(s), restricting feature, extreme tendencies, etc.

Right now, this world no hospital to treat this kinds of illness, everybody need pay attention--- depend on oneself.

Own thinking function may be normal or abnormal, this is the first level of issue.

The second level is that anyone to analyze something who need knowledge or "known" (messages, information). A general rule is that one's knowledge would limit one's quality of analysis. ---This can be called a theorem:

Knowledge limits.

As you knew the "knowledge limit theorem", and you also knew the range and precision of knowledge which be required for related issues. What to do, how to do is clear.

A theorem is that:---Fools don't know himself is a fool.

This is a conditional theorem, in general, most people go on thinking within his or her capacity to think, impossibility or no opportunity to touch outside of his or her capacity to think. In this way, most people have always been limited in a scope to think, impossibly can discover own thinking ability what level or own thinking scope what size.---Most people cannot find that, which is an exact existence, the ability of thinking is always has a "cannot".

That's why fools don't knows himself is a stupid. Except, someone does that "self-training" often.

If you know the theorem and you knew your own range of knowledge, the situation of thinking functions, you will know how to do.

So everyone treats himself, must understand that need an attitude of objective and detached, modesty are necessary.

We should be good at objectively examining ourselves and scientifically, systematically observing the system of ourselves.

Once a series of behavior problems occur, need to check the system, to test the main function, and finally to fundamentally solve the problems.

Look at others objectively, scientifically and systematically, same above.

If something goes wrong within our social system, or our social system is not good enough, or Power to control our country or society its behaviors are not good enough, or our society it is not safe enough.--- There are many reasons for those problems.---But in this chapter, to think only one reason is considered -

--Man, (men) have been problems:

1. This product should belong to the highest level and does not reach the high level.

2. The basic system, the most primitive system is not perfect.

3. The usual person has not reached the standard, has not reached of enough "Human Content", has not met the criteria, index which has been set up by the Creator or Nature.

This chapter only considers one content: the Person.

There is a principle of more realistic and more popular, this truth through the above contents can be proved to be common sense:

When everyone takes a vote to elect, and everyone's thinking function has been changed in mutation, no meaningful at this time of the vote.

To study of the situation of a country or studying of a society, need to survey each individual thinking functions firstly.

Everybody has to realize the healthy, sane Human Thinking Function. Because---you know.

Chapter 3

Unit of Social Activity

Section 1 The Real Situation

A person is the most basic Unit of Social Activity, and the Units are made by people, even man and an equipment is an unit too which is another kind of Unit. The following "Units of Social Activity" mostly refer to Units (combinations) which constituted by people.

Each Unit of Social Activity is a system which produced by its main function. (there are not that people's main functions add together simply.) The main function and working principle of the system are relatively complex, can only be analyzed in detail to each one if need.

In general, just a combination of two people, it means that everyone (two) must be tolerant and humble, that is, lose himself to a certain extent to each one. As more people formed an organization, the situation became more complex and each self-loses more. This moment, the common's principles of the organization will enhance and generated a vitality of the organization, and then a new life of an organization will be born. This life, which does not have the physiological indicators like the usual life, is the result of various factors, and its forces was gathered by various factors, to it cannot be underestimated.

There are many kinds of Units, such as on social activities, economic activities, recreational activities, etc.--- Are not the contents of this chapter.

In this chapter, only Special Units of Social Activity is discussed.

In the last 2,000 years or more, a kind of Units of Activity which has the goal is taking the Power, it has been highlighted. This kind of Units of Social Activity have the superficial characteristics:

1. Must be has a theory. (Maybe science or

theology or mystery)

2. To be an organization, composed of people. (Or religious organizations or political organizations)

Such Units of activity are often represented as religious organizations or political party organizations. But, however, not all religious organizations or political parties can become such Special Units of Social Activities.

This Special Unit of Social Activity which has a theory, the theory also has three important signs on the surface. The system of theory which has the main contents are usually talks about:

1. "Man, should be---."

2. "Human society, should be---."

3. Someone also concerned that "what is the creator," and "what is the basic principles of nature".

There seems to be nothing wrong on the surface. But, not.

The followings are only surface phenomenon which can reveal all the substantive problems:

1. There is a solemn ceremony to one join the organization, leading to a clear distinction

between members and non-members.

2. Members of this organization have been taught of their dedication for their organization.

3. A member if withdraw from the organization will be in danger.

When people examine and examine again to the above three characteristics in detail, would know, should know, this moment, without considering their content of the theory, will get the following judgment when only examining those three characteristics:

1. The vitality of organization has been generated.

2. Its members appear to be the living cells of the organization.

To think in reverse: If you have an organization like this firstly, and then you can free to find a theory on the shelf to inject the theory into the organization. How will to be? The simulated answer will tell you that the organization can still surviving and still evolving to the extreme.

At this time, it still does not consider its ideology and theory, but only considers its organizational structure, which has its own possibility and tendency towards extreme development.

So, what's the value about this organization's ideology or theory?

With just a little bit of meaning, its theory of thought will define the type of behavior of its organization.

However, the thought and theory consider about "people, how should", "the human society, how should", the contents, coupled with the organization's own characteristics, obviously, the organization will intervene in the social order, to seize, to control of Social Power.

---Usurp Power, it is the group's or organization's goal, it is the organization's behavioral peculiarity.

The goal, is not had published the "goal", the real peculiarity which never show(ed) on any file.---those are only on facts.---Unfortunately, people seem like that don't to pay attention to these facts, only pay attention to their theory.

This Special Unit of Social Activity is characterized

by seeking Power. Its goal usually belongs to the organization which can do so in spontaneously, its members don't know.

The theory of organization mainly has two categories, 1 --- if it is a "theistic" theory, it to be that "everything for the sake of god." 2 --- If it's theory of "science", to be "everything for science, from science".

Its members in this kind of organization, first of all, the thinking function caters to the regulation of the organization, and then the superficial "active behavior", in fact, no. Their Faith Function and Sense of Mission Function in their brains have mutated to the point that "everything is for the organization".

The role model who among its members generally is a leader may regard as both "theoretical authority" and "organizational authority".---Right or wrong, it doesn't matter, it's a superficial fact.

As to Human Thinking Functions, one of the Faith Function can induce people to focus on more than its own life scale: the contents of the distant past, the distant future, until the ultimate question, the ultimate truth, the ultimate fact.---There is no doubt that this is enough to prove that mankind is great creature and that there is no limit to its future.

So, about the source of this function can let people have a reason to make such guess, this function maybe was the Creator or Nature has sent a line to mankind, for humans to find the ultimate truth, let the human to be forever.

Based on the fact, this consideration to theism or atheism or any scientific theory, to explore the creator or, to explore the ultimate truth, to be worthy, can be respect, because is that for ultimate truth, this is the important thing, to try in any way be worth.

But, reality not. The great Human Thinking Function, had, has, have been deserted, damaged. Someone using the great function on to take something whose wanted.

The main theoretical questions will be explained in more detail in the chapter "Faith Function Knowledge System". Here is only a brief description,-

--The Units has the theory of the important content is （was） in a hypothesis. The theistic, atheistic, or scientific, all are "hypothetic".---The problems are not those, are this:

1. The attributes of the hypothesis are not clearly be defined and are often believed to be true, even forced to be true.

2. Any theory only meaning that is combined with a group of people to build a rigorous organization.

At present, such units of activity are still generated or die freely, and do what randomly without control.

Not many organizations can have survived for more than hundreds years, and are merely few of them have occupied the Nodes of Order, or can took (take) Power.

This kind of units of activity once have the ability, no matter whether it has control of state Power will lose no time to create conflict, such as, religious conflicts, political conflict, the conflict of civilization, the class conflict, and so on forth.

In another hand, any such conflict must be manipulated by such Unit of Social Activity.---This is the theorem.

This kind of units once controls the state Power or they control society, it will control people's thought, damage Human Thinking Function.---This is a theorem too.

It at least, to damage two of thinking functions:

1. Control people's Faith Function and limit the belief products.

2. Control people's Sense of Mission Function, limit the hierarchies of the Sense of Mission Function and limit the directions of the Sense of Mission Function.

This kind of units of activity if build a Power or hold a Power, the Power must be a dictatorship.--- This is the theorem.

Section 2 Scientifically Treat, Deal

Above, for this kind of units of description is brief, about the Units of Social Activity and it control society, which have only a few pivotal contents. Knowing this is a prerequisite for dealing such problems scientifically.

The following final judgment is only in relation to the previous details:

No unit or organization of social activities has the right to require its members to fight for the organization's life, no one has the right to require their members to die for them. (Except, the national armed forces.)

Any organization, by definition or in effect causes its members to die or fight for their organization's life. --- It is anti-human.

This obviously is a strange phenomenon, the causes of this phenomenon can be omitted, after all, this regulation is not in conformity with the humanity, does not conform to the god or "gods", do not accord with the basic meaning of Nature, do not conform to the general national law, do not conform to the science or pseudoscience. But, however, these kind of phenomenon are often, usual, widespread, why? This is a big question, this book cannot to answer.

Therefore, people should pay special attention to those---when who join a organization or a group by formal and serious ceremony,---The danger of society has lurked, as to the man maybe. And pay special attention to those---the generating of any Special Unit of Social Activity.

At present, the choice of lawmaking should be at least one:

1. Forceful the ban, forcefully prohibits to the kind of Units.

2. Compulsive registration. Compulsively order them to publish the relevant documents about the actual strength of the organization.

Popularize common knowledge about the

physiological functions of Faith and Sense of Mission.

Generally speaking, leaders of this Special Unit of Social Activity, to be a man of strong Faith Function, Sense of Mission Function, they are respected. But, their think function is a deformity at the same time, it is also lamentable. From the point of view of treating and saving people, they are severe and urgent patients, and they deserve special treatment.

They undermine people's thinking function, not by a design, but by blind action and ignorance. Although they may have read a lot of (deformed or great or strange) texts, that doesn't help them understand the basics. (A reminder: usually is that master garbage knowledge or incorrect knowledge more difficult than to master correct knowledge) Of course, their thinking function has been an illness as to treatment was, is, will very difficult.---For this requires specialized expertise, to do.

For the general public, popularize the common sense need achieve such a degree:

1. Anyone has the thoughts of "man, should be",

"human society, should be", and anyone has such a guess about the Creator, Nature.---It's a biological common sense.

2. Everyone has the ability to formulate religious theories and put together political theories. Everyone also has the ability to establish religious organizations or political party.---This is not a mysterious ability.

3. Everyone has the right to consider the Creator or ultimate truth. This right, qualification comes from the Creator, from the ultimate truth. No individual or group has the right to deprive your this gift, and no one is allowed to limit it.

4. Keeping your own Faith Function in healthy and sane, you're not far from the Creator.

Democratic countries need to popularize common sense:

1. This Special Unit of Social Activity has not yet seized state Power, and that is why democracy exists.

2. Once this kind of Special Unit of Social Activities

gains state power, the democratic system immediately is over, and, must be the alienation of Human Thinking Functions.

However, this Particular Unit of Social Activity, which is still active in democratic countries and, it is associated with some of the chaos.

Also, it is impossible for authoritarian countries to popularize such knowledge, such physiological knowledge. Therefore, the popularization of democratic countries will have model effect and infiltrating effect.

Religious or political theories can continue to be studied, and religious or political organizations can continue to exist. These are of particular importance to mankind. However, due to the dissimilation of its organizational structure, this kind of organizations loses the attribute of theoretical research and for this it is loses the necessity of existence.

Although an alienation seems to be more aggressive, it can be successful for a while, but it won't always, and it will eventually destroy the organization itself. ---The Divinity Stick or the Party Stick who seems never to think so objectively.---But, after all, it's a science, it's Social Science.

Chapter 4

The Power

Section 1 Truth of Power and Theoretical Model

The Power control society or command state society, whatever, it is called what name, it is extremely powerful and can be done of lots things in many ways.

It is so hard to count what it provides to the top Power holders, as this the Power holders are surprised.

Throughout world history, the top Power holders have often tried to label themselves as "the divine right of Kings".

This is a down-to-earth indication, they are already feeling disproportionate to their ability, because of the enormous capacity of Power compared to their personal ability.---They are in a little guilty.

Power is a mystery, but, is not the mystery as they understood. It does come from a predetermined cause indeed, that is, it has a natural attribute, it has a reason that Creator preset. (However, a predetermined reason is exists.)

Now try to summarize that human beings must have two kinds of productive relations because of Human Thinking Function:

1. The relationship of between the knowledge produce and use.

2. The relationship of between the produce and use of material wealth.

Under these two types of social relations are various complex Subsystem of Social Relations. These must require an Order, which was, is, will must create Order's Nodes.

Power, was, is, will always from the Nodes of

Order.

The force of Order and the social relationships, which situations it is can be calculated and described digitally.---Readers can to try. May you do a rough calculation, will be knowing the Power what is.

At least, on the surface, Power has the supreme controlling force and governing force. Those who fight for Power is competing for the supreme controlling force and governing force. About the controlling force and governing force be used for what? It includes people's understanding of Power.

Since the written history, the Power is has been enjoyed by the holders, which is a major content in the history.

Once an individual or a group controls the Power of a society or a state, Power becomes the best prize. This kind of Power is Private Power, Enjoying Type Power.---A Individual or a group to place personal willing on the Power, which is also called dictatorship often.

The same kind of Powers in this historical stage is marked with different characteristics, which is the same kind of Powers can be described by three names: Dictatorial Power, Private Power, and Enjoying Type Power. But, the Enjoying Type Power , this name can show main peculiarity.

The process of Power from small to large started from the Power of the family, followed by clan, ethnic group, villages and so on.---From the point of view of the process to see, the Power should be that to give the people "care" or "service".---This characteristic should exist. But it's not in fact.

It seems that the more "theoretical" its Power holders have emphasized, the Power more brutal. Whether theistic or scientific, the more "theoretical" the power was, is intensively reduces the kindness to its members. Is this a theory of Power got a problem, or is the theory of grab Power which has never been human nature? (Hope reader to answer.)

The history of Private Power was changed in the 16th century. Europeans began to understand and enforce limit on Power.

They did, there are actually two objective consequences:

1. Cut down Power actions.

2. Reduce the contents of Power give the enjoyments to the holder.

Both of these items have great significance.---The former need not to say, (but, the problems have been buried.), in the latter, the contents of the Power it to provide the holders with enjoyments, if enjoyments are increases or decrease, which affects the intensity of the Power Struggle.

From human nature to the nature of Power, the theoretical model of Power can be interpreted, and then the problems can be seen:

1. Power exists because human need it. Its obligation is for human safety. (secondly is else Units of social activity---.)

2. Power exists for the need of Order.

3. Power exists for the need of various social relations.

It can be seen that Power is of (which has) great value and important responsibility.

Because the Power (almost) is the Node of Order, its force can be generated from Node of Order, its energy has born from all kinds of relationships. So, individual or a group capacity cannot match of it. It's easy for a group or for someone to take something. But for human society, it's just a partial using Power.

Usually, this Node is always occupied by a system or a group or a person, and since then, the capacity of a system or a group or a person which has been strengthened immediately and, which is so-called a social Power, government Power, etc. Although it has lots of name, the quality of the system, the group, the person will affect the quality of power.

This book (sometimes) said the Power is (was) born for human society, exist for human society---. In short, it is neither good nor bad. History and present have only two questions:

Who is using the Power?

What does Power do?

All of problems can be hided in these two questions.

Section 2   Dictatorial Powers

The long period of autocratic Powers is the sleep period of human nature. The Make-Stupid and slaughtering function of dictatorial Powers have caused of so many disasters, for thousands of years of this Power act recklessly is human progress has slowed.

Someone or some group was, is, will to seize Power, protecting Power and enjoying the Power, such things become social mainline.

As to Power's activities caused of the killings, are prevalent around the world and, have the alarming record. An Enjoying Type Power eventually set up on less than one over ten of the survivor's head, such things occurs, it is not only ancient, modern, maybe in future, in our world.

How to seize Power? How to protect Power? How to enjoy Power?---Someone is struggling to find the way, someone patiently produces the scheme.---For this are often called "achievements of civilization", "Religious theory" "political party theory" "political theory" "social science" and so on.

What is the Power used for? To enjoy.

The powerful controlling force and governing force of Power, firstly has (have) been dwarfed and then be recognized. Thereafter, this Power is an award to the striver, to the winner, after it belongs an individual or group, its attribute is the Private Power. Its functions are to provide enjoying products for the possessor.

Note: If (in fact) researchers to all kinds of the state Powers, wholly were, are similarly called "public power", it is to confuse right and wrong, it don't possess the basic precision to research.

Enjoying Type Powers, Private Powers, have natural exclusiveness.---So, it must be an autarchy.

Although dictatorships come in many forms, corporate dictatorships, ideological systems, family dictatorships, and so on, the ultimate form is individual dictatorship.

The nature of Enjoying Type Powers are of the same, and the autocracy main contents are same. However, in different backgrounds and at different times, there will be different forms, vertical human history, and the horizontal world, Enjoying Type Power has its own characteristics no change.

If the leader of the Power pays special attention to the role of mind or some theory, and he can show basic integrity, whether true or false, the Power has the desire to expand and the dictatorial Power has an aggressiveness. How big of the offensive capability is another matter.

If the head of Enjoying Type Power is unlikely to attain the highest level of superstition, that is, dignity is impossible to reach the top, he will pay attention to the technology of sharing power as a benefit.

If the leader of Enjoying Type Power only pay attention to personal benefits, their sharing groups have the characteristic of interest alliance or criminal alliance.

The Powers with such a few rules will have a lot of

strange forms.

Power, this moment, the social function is compressed.

Enjoying Type Power using its absolute advantage of the enjoyments, can be always to absorb talents, to create talents and to allot manpower. So that, the society using enjoyments as a general value judgment and code of conduct, and does not allow some people to enjoy Power as a supplementary code of conduct.

People's thoughts on social reality, human relations, even including research institutions of thoughts, religious institutions or called social sciences, were occupied by the Enjoying Type Power to enjoy.

Enjoying Type Power its enjoyments include, but is not limited to, dignity, wealth, service, and sacrifice.

Since the enjoying goods include human, it is naturally to apply the methods of make-stupid, schemes of weakening, the deceptions are only a complementary method to the people.

The consequences of make-stupid must be lots of strange forms.

Influential and dazzling form are two categories, one of them is Private Power made both stupid and weak to people at the same time, synchronous accomplish. The other is that although was made the stupid people are not weak, but pay attention to keeping the people to be ignorance, strong, barbarous.

The latter often produced patriotic elegies for other Private Powers in the fight for Private Power's something.

Being stupid is all social problem. Power holders who enjoy Power on all levels, on the other hand, people who have absolutely no Power to enjoy, but, the miracle is that all of they can understand this is a rationality.

People who hold Power at the top they feel cheated without protest. They can use a sense of mission to mask self-interest and can fulfill personal preferences. They may really think that they raised the stupid people, they really thought is that if no them himself the people are of nothing, they really thought is that they to be represent civilization, represent people and so on. The people have no Power, have no ability to feel cheated, they believe that they deserve it.

In fact, their schemes of make-stupid and deception of make-weak to their citizens, are not deliberate intentions, there is no conspiracy theory, but, it is an instinctive deliberate.

When the Power holder implements the scheme of make-fool, the scheme of make-weak, deceptive scheme, they are, will have lots of talents from all sides to help them and, interpret the schemes to people.

People will also be patient and truly understanding, flexible to accept those methods and programs, are often spontaneously eliminating the sober one, the questioning, or the various "heresies".

This operation system on human society to human beings, in theoretical deduction, humans are meaningless, and the model is the worst way to prove futile.

"Enjoy", will be cannot felt to enjoy the fun eventually, it could be simplified to the person himself be species form, however, just because of historical reasons, its form be more special, the role be same as the queen of bee, the king of ant.

The highest state of being the victims will be not feeling bullied, crushed, enjoyed, no pain anymore. Caused by it, it be reduced to a functional form of a species, and its role be equivalent to worker ants or soldier ants.

Human Thinking Function, because of no use and no longer exists, humans also like a low-level creature, the body and low-level intelligence be one-time casting type be completed, and then people can be on "autopilot" to complete the whole journey of life.

Of course, it's not that serious at this time, but efforts in this direction have never stopped. Even in some areas, there have been physiological consequences.

Therefore, there should be a basic judgment on such powers: It is anti-human.

This kind of Powers, in terms of the function of enjoyment, is always unfair and has always no motivation to pursue fairness.

In the view of private nature, this kind of powers belongs to the individual and belongs to the individual's free will.

In terms of its autocratic contents, such Powers be bound to damage people's thinking function, especially act on the Faith Function and the Sense of Mission Function.

The most deadly danger of this Power is that---it impairs Human Thinking Function.

With the general knowledge revealed by genetics, if being damaged of Human Thinking Function which situation once enters the genetic program, human history over immediately.

Today, the end of dictatorship to this meaning is not just because of its brutality, it is not just because of its unfairness or its corruption. It is to protect the basic security of mankind.

The conclusion is indisputable, these Powers must be get rid of.

This kind of Powers has no needs for reform. The so-called reform is that to make it better use of the fruits of the times and the democratic system, it can be let dictatorship make-stupid to people scientifically.

The diversity of the national system or the diversity of international community must be based on the premise of the democratic system, which can not include the anti-human system or "anti-system system".

If someone be entangled in historical reasons, in short, let it understand the simple truth: human beings need security and human beings must move forward.

These principles are simple and clear, so, how to end dictatorship?

The scientific scheme(s) be aimed at the Human

Thinking Function.

In today's world, in some places Human Thinking Function under the control of dictatorships it has generally been impaired:

1. Self-help scheme, in theory, does not exist. Occasionally, a dictatorship collapse suddenly, the people suddenly have a free choice, no good results, because their thinking functions have been a malformation.

2. In any rescue plan, the first step is to restore people's thinking function. This is an indispensable step.

Thinking function recovery work and its staff:

1. Professionals should be almost from outside, from democratic areas that is correct in theory.

2. The human elite among dictators, may be, that is a complementary theory.

It is hard to say which one is better, after all, the principle is: 1.) The purpose must be clear and the plan should be published. 2.)This is a professional and technical job, which is equivalent to popularizing popular science knowledge. 3.) This work is that go beyond the topics of "civilization", "custom", "tradition", "national view" and "religion", etc.

In this way, the staff can work safely and exit safely.

Section3 Democratic Power

Democratic states, democratic institutions, Public Power, or called Responsible Type Power, however, which can be have been created hundreds of years old.

Democratic institution, it perhaps comes from a providence. The reasons seem that people do not know it true value, the total value, however, it has already appeared.

Those kind of cognitive error, resulting in different practical consequences. But, definitely not by democratic (political) theory to it can generating.--- Because the democratic theory is incomplete, and practice guided by democratic theory fails more than succeeds.--- Now, around the world, failures are still happen often to build a democratic institution.

It is true, after all, it seems that there are only a few dozen decent democratic states, and they are still riddled with internal contradictions and abuse one's power. The rest are hardly worth mentioning, and their reality is so dire that they have actually become an excuse for the dictatorship to continue.

The primary form of Responsible Type Power, as a matter of fact, had indeed emerged in the distant past and is still frequently present at various stages of history.

But it did not develop, or it did not have the opportunity to grow into the scale of Power of social significance, and it did not dominate society for a long time.

The reasons for this are truly curious.

We can do this backward to think. At the beginning of civilization, starting point of wisdom or/and knowledge,---. It's random who gets there first to control Power, maybe, there can be any kind of randomness at the most primitive starting point, Human Thinking Function be capable of accepting any randomness and still can go the right way, and any randomness will cause one of the ultimate characteristics of human behavior.

Why human beings, through tyranny, dictatorship (Enjoying Type Power, Private Power,)? maybe for this, can form the memory of the culture, can erect the fence of prohibition with the achievements of wisdom.

It is fair to say that it is a random mistake that brings Private Power into the body of human society and occupy the position of coordination center. This determines that human beings must be gorge the evil consequences and then know the good results, and purify the truth of human society with the lessons of blood.

When humans really wake up or fully recover, must be firmly and faster pace go forward.

The logical inference is that Responsible Type Power can come into being at any time from the original starting point to the future, but it is more difficult to come into the "Power" at the peak of the civilization of Enjoying Type Power.

When civilization or culture, tradition, wisdom, knowledge, etc. have problems, the society is more necessary and needs a Responsible Type Power. Although the Responsible Type Power at this time may or may not be efficient, it is still the best supporting force to society. How if chose the Enjoying Type Power? It could be an inferior in quality, it behaviors be cruel more. Any inferior Public Power, must be better than no or any Enjoying Type Power. It's hard to explain with facts, below are a few reasons.

Democratic Power, Public Power, Responsible Type Power or democratic system have many advantages. In short, there is only one that can make Human Thinking Function healthy and sane.(In the beginning, even with a small probability, a small number.)

Only this one is enough, that is, for this one can make a positive conclusion about Democratic Power or democratic system: it is qualified to exist.

In fact, it is, for this reason, cause other related consequences: people's creativity, social vitality, scientific and technological achievements. And so on.

Now, the questions are that to the Responsible Type Powers are on what level? What problems they have to solve?

Their understanding of the Person is not accurate enough.

Since there are no requirement for the Human Thinking Function, for example, the "freedom" of man is immature, which is equivalent to allowing the freedom of children's standards for adult's.---This is obviously ridiculous. So, if is lower the "Person Content" the standard of freedom, how? The answer, the reader knows.

This kind of problems, this kind of defects can lead to other problems, of course, such as high crime rate, illegal organizations too lots, and so on.

After all, among democracy, the Human Thinking Function is safe. Even if it is not a precise goal, it can naturally produce many (little) people with sound thinking functions. But, if have a goal of making everyone thinking function healthily and sane, there is very different.

That is why democracy needs to be improved.

Responsible Type Powers have no comprehensive attention on have already been existed of social relations.

There are two main types of social relations: 1.) The social relation of knowledge produce and use. 2.) The social relation of material wealth produce and use.

Given the lessons of authoritarian power, there is the talk of a "small government, big society", and limiting power that are fashionable academic ideas.---Those are not a scientific point of view.

Control is not blind control. But, first thing is that pay attention to every social relation, even someone needs to control someone not.

If you don't know what knowledge on society is producing, what knowledge is being use. The consequences are predictable.

If the guiding role of material wealth is not considered at all, and material wealth continues to be guided by "enjoy", for these, what are consequences? This can lead to the Responsible Type Power itself lost responsibility, lost direction.---This kind of facts are usually.---This a big problem.

Social relations are huge and complex. On the premise of comprehensive attention, it is not difficult to treat someone scientifically, to manage something scientifically.

Public Powers, (Democratic Power, RTP) or democratic systems, which have the advantage in term of providing contents, and which have the problems, the conclusion is: it should be improved.

Chapter 5

Hypothesis Knowledge System

Section 1 Real Situation

As for the classification of knowledge, it is usually classified according to the objects of knowledge, as there are mathematics, physics, history, geography, etc. There are also methods of classifications, so there are scientific knowledge and non-scientific knowledge.

This book talk about classification of knowledge which is classified by Thinking Function. In this way, we can see the original characteristics of knowledge and its basic direction of action.

It is easier to understand the purpose of knowledge by classifying in this way. Indirectly see it, the knowledge comes from the ultimate truth and points to the ultimate truth.

There are mistakes and gaps (blank space) in the during of growths of knowledge. There are many reasons why human behavior is wrong or/and meaningless. Only by knowledge theory, it may be that wrong knowledge induces or there is no correct knowledge for guidance.

With this classifying method, there will be a dozen types of knowledge systems. This book only enumerates three knowledge systems: the Hypothesis Knowledge System, the Logical Knowledge System, and the Sense of Mission Knowledge System. (Faith Function Knowledge System, Logic Function Knowledge System, Sense of Mission Function knowledge System.)

Use these three examples to try to make the following effect:

1. Point out relevant knowledge of major issues. Solve specific problems in related areas.

2. Lead people to think: 1.) Set the purpose of this function. Or 2.) The purpose of the function.

At first, with Human Thinking Function, and then has the human corresponding behavior:

1. The Faith Function is existed firstly, later, have the Faith Knowledge System.

2. This knowledge, like all others knowledge, has a growth process: 1.) The total amount increases without rules. 2.) Systematize.

Activities of Faith Function can be reclassified:

1. The Hypothesis.

2. Fantasy, ideal, hope.

3. The plan.

According to this classification, some problems are exposed. People may have a wonder, is this knowledge? (Does that make sense?) This is the preschool children often childish performance! The answer is yes, it's knowledge, and it's important knowledge. It has also significant meaning.

The range of activities of function or scope of knowledge is that:

The Ultimate Truth---The Ultimate Truth.

Everyone has been active and uninhibited since

childhood showing this function. As one gets older, this function still exists, but it becomes more cautious. For adults who show this kind of thinking freely will be condemned as "babble" or "lie".

Now, the practical effect of this function can be discussed:

1. The hypothesis is the first step in the pursuit of certainty.

2. After hypothesis (may, to presume), maybe has hypotheses chains and hypothesis conclusions.

3. If the hypothesis is true, the chains and conclusions can be repeated on using.

In spite of the functional effects, it is a complicated work. This chapter and the following two chapters are only part of the relevant contents.

From the perspective of human beings, the Faith Function is to explore the unknown world, and also has specific features, it has a "call for help " function.

To believe or not to believe without argument that is an essential feature of this function. It provides a wide range of thinking, from the past to the future, to the ultimate truth.

The quality of thinking is elementary, but not ridiculous. Its attributes do (did) what have "hypothetical" features, but this is preparation for an argument. As far as the "issue" be concerned, it is the first step in this "assumption" that uncovers (relevant) everything.

For all people in general, if don't set assumptions, would not pursue certainty, and cannot get out of zero.

All kinds of knowledge begin with assumption(s).

The use of "hypotheses" by a specific individual does not necessarily lead to the initiation of a "knowledge", because the objects are too specific and too narrow to constitute a series of knowledge. But sometimes, it's easy to produce a plan.

Fantasy, ideal, hope, is the cradle of planning.

Fantasy, ideal, hope and so on all have the attribute of "hypothetical" in essence. Only some of them will be grand plans, while some others may be on the road of logical deduction.

Planning is also a type of hypothesis.

There is a risk of error in using the belief function.

With this function, the error rate is difficult to make statistics. Just said, through a specific individual, their life by Faith Function guide ideas, for the most part, there is no difference between right and wrong, after all, most of all be abandoned, forgotten.

As far as a specific individual is concerned, even a child will not easily put all his "ideas" into practice and know how to avoid risks. Most "assumptions" are discarded without being taken seriously. But the overall impact of this feature is not to be underestimated.

For a person, if you want to test their character, you can make a judgment after checking their fantasies, ideals and plans.

This thinking function is essential for all mankind:

It determines the ultimate direction of human beings. Because the function considers that more than a natural person of the scale of the individual life, (with human life, survival rule is unable to understand) the contents involved in the past, including the origin, including the distant future. An individual, cannot relate to all of them, but as far as the total human population is concerned, that is already the case.

The human plan seems to be in the making. Even taking into account the destructive Power of extremist groups, human beings have been relentlessly seeking the ultimate goal.

The process of using this function has (until now) revealed several major problems:

1. The ultimate target is (almost) identified by some religious organizations or political parties in a strong hypothesis. Their so-called "planning" is not based on a solid basis, not serious enough, it belongs to the ideal category.

2. It is tempting to describe their ideal in beautiful language and exquisite performance art, but it is an ideal yet, which is less serious than plan.

3. Their planning seems logical and serious, but it

is still a kind of hypothesis after all. Just looking at its starting point and target, could be know, they not enough to call it a planning.

Comparison of Faith Function and Logical Function:

1. Faith comes before Logic.

2. Faith is more macro.

3. Logic is more practical.

All kinds of scientific knowledge are inseparable from the one of the earliest "hypothesis" or "hypotheses", although the various kinds of "hypothesis" come true, cannot treat as the same, however, human "certainty", source of knowledge is come from the "hypothesis" from the beginning.

Individuals, when one is in a desperate situation, will spontaneously set up the "hope", and then move in the direction of "hope". One will also seek blessing and prayer, pray for the "god, gods" to bless oneself.---This kind of behavior, guided by the function of thinking, it has not changed much since ancient times.

"Hope" still exists, the content(s) of hope has changed little, and the difference in its content is related to personal experience and knowledge.

There had been some changing in the concept of "god, gods" of all, which is related of the scientific development and technological knowledge. The idea of the "universe" in terms of scientific knowledge, which is impacted of old ideas, but it doesn't matter. The true meaning be defined only by the actual requirements of the person who be present.

The "hope", the search for protection, the struggle for life and will not come to nothing. Every success will make a person lifetime unforgettable. The account of this experience is a primitive condition for the development of such knowledge.

But, the prayer is useful? After all, this behavior is universal, and it has been using by everyone since ancient times.

This book believes that prayer is useful, which is a function of "calling for help". The problem is that you can't prove how it works now, so it's a guess.

"Hope," the search for blessings, the struggle for

life and all of which often do wonders. On the one hand, such cases are easily mythologized. On the other hand, it is true that Creator heard the cry for help and intervened directly, leading to miracles. (Guess) This is also the intention of setting up this function.--- "Call for help".

After all, when Faith Function be changed (malformation or low level), the "call for help" could be useless.

---How can make a "call for help" be effective? Big question! Now, no a professional institute to research it, all of they are busy on also. That's the issue of belong experts, need experts. (Hope readers try.)

People cherish own (their) Faith Function and protect the Faith function in a healthy, safe, it is also profound meaning.

Section 2 General direction of the whole system

So, let's take all the assumptions, all the hypothesis points, even some assumptions became true, all of they put into consideration, it can be roughly seen that one of the main functions of Faith Function is to point the way for humanity to seek its Creator. Humans are always to do so.

Section 3   Avoid risks scientifically

The belief function has great value and direct significance to individuals and human society:

1. The belief function will point out people's lifelong goals and behavior patterns. To human society is same.

2. The absence of belief function or the impairment of belief function it means that who is the loss of basic human characteristics or been reduced of "Human Inclusion", "Human purity".

Therefore, religious organizations or political party organizations should know these basic common senses, (if) made, make "knowledge" complicated and the complex without basic common sense, which is of no real significance to human society.

Professional studying of Faith Function Knowledge, neither feigning to be a god nor pretending to be science, should start from primitive simplicity:

1. Truly understand what is assumed and what is true. (It's not easy.)

2. It is correct to make assumptions in pursuit of certainty, but do not make false assumptions fulsomely.

3. Dare to label "assumptions" professionally.

Because everyone has the Faith Function, everyone must has "hypothetical" thinking. Although specific individuals will have a specific threshold, the amount of the majority of people be bound to hit a "person, how should", "human society, how should", and, these "hypothetical" thinking, the total must be covering completely.---This is the source of religious theory and political party theory.

Individuals should be careful when applying

hypothesis thinking. The "theoretical" team should also be careful about applying hypothesis theories. Social application of hypothesis thinking or even systematic "hypothetical" theory should be more careful.

The safe approach is that a planning or a theory who be validated and conform with specific procedures.

At present, quality of the relevant professional organizations may not very good, quite simply, people do not pay attention to their own thinking function, do not pay attention to improve their thinking function, this is the most basic Unit of Social Activity has quality defect, and from the most basic Units which constitute anything, the quality is not optimistic.

Imagine that a person with a very low "Person Content" telling others what to do. It's a joke. It's not a joke, it's the beginning of a disaster, to have a group of people with very low levels of "Human Purity" telling people what to do.

If everybody's belief function, can act normally, the total number of religious organization, political party organization should be more than 100 times more than at present, and each one has the academic characteristic.

At present, the total number of religious organizations and political parties in areas where controlled by the democratic system they are already lots, but there are still on quality problems and academic status problems.

Now, dictatorship control areas, the religious organizations, political party organizations already very rare, and they are scrambling to find Power, trying to make a living by deceit and violence make its organization better.

By taking the actual situation of Faith Function as an indicator, we can detect the relevant problems of a society:

1. (If) its hypothesis points are not even, its society has at least one operator. (Malicious or unintentional)

2. (If) there is only one kind of belief products, this society is a deformed society. The Faith Function of this society has been deformed.

It is enough to examine faith institutions by looking at only one of their behavioral traits:

As long as it is forced to sell its belief products, it will certainly damage people's belief function. Such institutions, whether they call themselves "theistic" or "atheistic" or "scientific", are essentially ignorant and unhelpful. In theory, it is atheistic and unscientific.

The current belief theory system, whether theistic or scientific (pseudoscientific), cannot withstand quantitative analysis. Therefore, such organizations should:

1. Continue your research modestly.

2. Give up violence and lies.

It must be remembering that this is not an attack on religious theory or political party theory. As mentioned above, belief theory includes religious theory and political party theory, which is of vital importance to human beings. But, need know the common sense and the basic principles firstly.

Nature, Creator, Human thinking Function, are not to be challenged.

Therefore, the essential content of "freedom of belief" should clearly include freedom of Faith Function safely, freely to use this function, and freely to use the products of faith.

Chapter 6

Logical Knowledge System

Section 1 Basic Structure

Because there's the Logical Function in Human Thinking Function, and then there's a Logical Function to apply. (logic function=logical function)

When the results of Logical Function application reach a certain scale, a logical knowledge system be (was) generated.

The feature of this functional application is quite obvious because it has a definite process: known --- reason---conclusion. It is especially clear for inspection.

The scope of action: known---new "known".

Because the Human Thinking Function and Logical Function are possessed by human brain, the use of such function, just like the function of the respiratory system or diet system, can be used without training (almost).

The so-called training is mainly focused on how to express clearly. This does not substantially change the Logical Function. Although training can make Logical Functions more fluid and more habitual, it can improve them.

At present, people's Logic Function is largely intact. And because the logical chain is easy to inspect, there is no problem with Logical Knowledge.

The Logical Knowledge System is like a magnificent building, and the building materials are extremely simple: known, reason and conclusion.

"Known" is the first important step.

Generally speaking, as long as the "known" can be done well, a moderate and accurate conclusion can be produced almost immediately.

The expansion of logical knowledge system as is the expansion of "known" quantity. If "known" can be increased, the logical building can be expanded.

The sources of "known" are extremely complex and the ways of taking Known are extremely complex.---Those are being on the contents of professional books.

As a matter of fact, people are not fully known of any "thing" or any "object", the so-called "known" is only refers to the situation that "known" can match the reason and conclusion.

In what circumstances a "thing" or "object" be defined as "known" and can be applicable; The original Known, in what case can been improved on an "accuracy", become a new "known".---These, it seems, not simple things. The "known" role and value are extremely important, for thousands of years, the great scientists among mankind, through continuous efforts, have left solid theoretical and physical achievements for future generations.

Section 2   The Development

Human Logic Function is physiological possessed, but it seems that only in the ancient Greek era began to produce systematic knowledge, in which the ancient Greek mathematical knowledge became the forerunner of various kinds of science. Then, after thousands of years of silence, it suddenly began to develop again, probably at the end of the Middle Century. (in sync with the emancipation of the mind, with the improvement of Human Thinking Function.) People so-called modern technology is actually only a few hundreds of years old.

The Logical Function of human has never changed. Why is it intermittent? The crucial first step--- "known", the Known has the key role and the known total amount would determine the expansion of Logical Knowledge System.

Any Known can arise, any decisive Known can be confirmed, the Logical Knowledge System expands immediately, and new scientific knowledge emerges immediately. These things are often happening within the scientific community.

In that "circle of scientific man", scientists can

improve the accuracy or find new one by accident.---These provide new categories for the next generations by new "known".---This is the problem of the expansion of the Logical Knowledge System too, that is, wastelands need, which have not been cultivated for a long time, where the fruits lots, they continue to flourish, to flourish intensively.

Modern scientific knowledge is expanding and refining on the one hand, on another hand scientific knowledge could be carried out in such an orderly manner, will sooner or later be fully cover on others functional knowledge systems. An age of reasonable mix together of all knowledge will come sooner or later. But, the question is now, when will that happen?

Look at only Faith Function or Sense of Mission Function, belief function more macro status, the sense of mission function seems to have the characteristics of the "obsessive-compulsive disorder", it's also can control something. The stability of the logic functions and the certainty of knowledge, this, make itself easy in the position of "tool". ---In fact, it's similar to this:

1. Scientific knowledge, serves the belief knowledge system, serves the sense of mission knowledge system, and the system of selfish desire knowledge.

2. Scientists, following products of faith, products of the sense of mission, products of self-interest.

3. Scientists are subordinate to Power.

This obviously greatly reduces the social benefits of logical function and logical knowledge system.

This is generally not easy to change, because the "dominant forces" do not want change, do not allow change, and the "dominant forces" always exist.

An opportunity is needed, and this opportunity leads to be a miracle: the Logical Knowledge System, which systematically questions each knowledge with logic rules, could be can improves the quality of the "dominant force" itself.

Section 3 Reminders

A society, a group, a person, each one has a regularity to Known, to knowledge. 1.) Necessarily produce contents of a stipulation. 2.) Cannot produce contents of a stipulation.

Known or serial Known can stipulate a direction, a roadway to society, to a group, to person.

Known or serial Known(s), they are not always, all, totally good, useful. Something, someone do (did) in mistake can be following correct known or serial known.

There seem that part of knowledge is a double-edged sword. Be restricted knowledge or / and that knowledge ceases to develop---it is harmful, perhaps like it did not occurring in the first place.

This danger is the results because unhealthy Power and harmful Units of activity.---People seem to have gotten used to the facts.

From the function theory, from the Human Thinking Function, can sure enough, the Real Theism and the Real Science Theory be consistent, because they all start from the reality and go to the ultimate truth.

The accumulation of knowledge to this day, we

are not enough to have a True Theism or a True Scientific Theory.

But the era of man's basic maturity did not seem far off.

To scientists this chapter has a reminder:

People including any scientists should to check own Faith Function and the Sense of Mission Function whether on perfect, or else, when you not perfect, even is only reduced "Human purity" yourself, also be damaging others more serious. No matter what you achieve in scientific achievements, after all, you must be a low-purity person.

Chapter 7

The sense of Mission Function Knowledge System

Section1 Practical Application

The Sense of Mission Function, like others thinking functions, has its own attentive direction, own method of analysis and judgment.

Over time, this knowledge systems be formed. Except the Logical Knowledge System, others knowledge systems are not rigorous enough, and the records, descriptions, and disseminating modes are not clear enough. Which is easy to be ignored and even suspected what exactly exist the authenticity of such knowledge.

The main function of the sense of mission which

lead anyone to be responsible for something. The direction, scope, and emphasis of the responsibility will be different due to different people, and people must be have different the induction of knowledge (experience, etc.).

Such knowledge can guide people, specific individuals, choosing what is worth taking on, and then decide how long and how much effort to take on that.

A person may have multiple responsibilities, and the cost to each one will be different even with some changes, for example, one lifelong goal may decide to mathematics, to solve some problems of mathematics, who also will have to be borne for family everything, but who can also chooses a particular team, decided not to give up every opportunity to the scene for the team a pep talk.--- These can exist in one person at the same time and can be regulated and implemented, even change someone, something by oneself.

The original effect of the function, it will induce human beings in all aspects can emerge the outstanding people.

Take the scientific knowledge of various categories as the example. Everyone who make outstanding contributions to science, who must be supported by a sense of mission.

The quality of the work will be very different, one is appointed or another one undertaken on a voluntary basis. In particular, the complex and difficult matters, which require long-term persistence, if can taking an achievement which only by those who do them with a sense of mission.

The Sense of Mission Function (or another) which can be reclassified into categories and hierarchies--- This chapter is only showing primary level.

The theoretical model of the simulation is like follows:

1. Any person may be responsible to any matter.

2. Each important thing deservedly has more than one person bear it.

3. Generally speaking, the person will choose a "project of great significance" and strive for it

in all one's life.

4. Everyone has at least one chosen that maybe will fight for it whole life. Also, still has other options as much responsibilities as possible.

5. Everyone chooses the option they even fight for it whole life, whether it is important or not, and whether it is worth. There are many judgments: 1.) The judgment of the majority. 2.) Self-judgment. 3.) Judgment on religious thought, political thought, and other thoughts. 4.) Power judgment.

Usually is that one believe(d) that has only a self-judgment to an obligation.--- On the surface, always; Deep down in the truth, that's never the case.

This model is a normal or theoretical society. This person's choice depends on relevant knowledge, and the quality of that knowledge is another issue. Whether this person can freely insist that his or her choice is an issue, the various social judgments of thought or power judgment and so on belong to different issues.---At least, seeming, the persons have options.---But, dictatorship times the dictatorship is always to assign or to appoint options.

The increased process of the sense of mission knowledge cannot be uniformly, comprehensive, which is the problem of knowledge itself. On the other hand, in the course of this process, there are some artificial priorities, which are the fatal problems in this process, such as for religious organization, political organization.

In general, the Sense of Mission Function and relevant knowledge are of great action. It can make human individuals evenly dispersed to endless "key points", and the progress of human society, because each "key point" has person(s) who with a sense of mission spirit, strong people, in the spirit of a sense of mission to promote the human social progress.

The reality is different than this theoretical model, the social problems or defects of the democratic system:

1. It is generally good that anyone is free to

choose a lifelong goal.

2. The drawback: Not everyone must be have a lifelong goal. Some people have give up, even no more, willingly.

3. For those who have already chosen a lifelong goal, make a statistic that if there are too many people who pursue "to enjoying type goods", it is this kind of knowledge has wrong. There are signs that something has goes wrong.

Dictatorial society social problems or defects:

The lifelong goal of human endeavor is defined by Power, which may be to fight for religious organizations, political party organizations.

On the one hand, the sense of mission knowledge reveals that there are a few "priorities", lacked of "key points". That is, people's sense of mission is generally monotonous, simplified and weak.

This is the general picture.

Section 2 Concerns Power

The Sense of Mission Function, generally to let people, in general, to choose "huge matters, important issue" to take responsibility, so this kind of status in the human social progress has an important action:

1. The top Power position is always the target be chosen by responsible people. The top Power holder must be people who with a strong sense of mission(if has).

2. Ideological studies with great social influence are inevitably interfered by those who with a strong sense of mission. Religious organizations, political party organizations and other leading figures must be people who with strong sense of mission(if have).

The knowledge system of the sense of mission and Sense of Mission Function always acts on the Nodes of Order and must be erect a Power. Therefore, it has built the Power to control the society, this process in history of writing has happened and, will continue.---This is only one aspect of the Sense of Mission Function made.

Specific personnel of religion or political party they are not only determined by the Sense of Mission Function, its own is a complex, integrated system,(the person as a system) comprehensive contents which must include: beliefs, desires knowledge system, logic knowledge system and so on.

When the Power be formed to control the society, the quality of Power itself and the quality of Power holder influence each other, and the situation is more complicated:

1. Power, which has accommodated the range of power holder, decides the types of Power holder it chooses(SMF).

2. The Power holder can change a certain extent and many aspects of Power (SMF).

These contents ultimately determine the benefits or disadvantage of Power to society.

The Power position is a typical representative. In fact, there are such problems in any position:

1. How likely is the job's self-regulation to evoke a

sense of mission?

2. In the series of posts, from top to bottom, the possibility of evoking of the Sense of Mission Function which is from strong to weak.

When a society is that, just the supreme Power location, and only for a special project, can pay people's sense of mission, which can be found the problems: A Power allow the Power characteristics of a sense of mission. To this, no sense of mission, no one has Sense of Mission Function almost. In fact, this situation be (is) that whole society lose sense of mission or Sense of Mission Function, or that, it have wholly been a malformation.

Generally speaking, the sense of mission of power holders are malformed, they must be wanton and can certainly create disasters. And its Selfish Function is arbitrary, in most cases, it merely creates a spectacle of corruption, it being noticed, it big problem is that type of the sense of mission has problem.

In any case, the Sense of Mission Function plays a vital role in controlling the Power of society.

The function of the sense of mission which has an only positive effect on power in early, original situations without side effect.

Long long time ago, controlling power of the family, controlling power of the ethnic group, the sense of mission function of the power figure was clear, its dedication and responsibility were obvious. Later, it gradually changed (may little), since then its function and knowledge system were in violation of its own value. It is impossible to find out when exactly it began.

If people play a responsible role in the Nodes of Order to build a Power, this path, starting with family and gradually goes to ethnic groups, villages, countries, and society,---obviously, it to be able to work hard and take responsibility---protecting and helping the weak, puniness. Therefore, the Power developed from this to control the Power of the state or society must be Public Power.--- This is clearly not the case.---Thousands of years was no Public Power in this world.

There are many problems in this chapter, which only consider the Sense of Mission Function.

Sense of Mission Function was, is always blend of beliefs, desires functions and so on, after began to complicate, this Sense of Mission Function again upon society with the power's means it saddle on social sense of mission, this time, is a type of mutation, social sense of mission was changed is of monotonous, simplified, harmful. Monotonous and simplified types are defined by the characteristics of Power and Power figures.

Therefore, when autocratic Power be born, they must create the malformation of the Sense of Mission Function, and the conditions on which can be the autocracy depends.---the malformation of a social sense of mission function. Since then, it has been easy for society to wander around within a defined type of dictatorship. So, one Power is collapsed, another be created, is roughly in line for thousands of years.

To examine the Power of a society or the social system of a society:

1. The Sense of Mission Function is an indispensable indicator.

2. The situation of the Sense of Mission Function

has a prescriptive effect on the social system, and has been stipulated a type.

3. The situation of the Sense of Mission Function has a definite effect on the vitality of this society.

The top power figures, the quality of their Sense of Mission Function may be affected or interfered by two categories:

1. Faith function knowledge system.

2. Selfish Desire Knowledge System.

Selfish Desire Function, was (is) the Creator has given senior creatures including human beings, as to the function can be self-preservation, because any rescue most timely rescue anyone be less their own, this is the first virtue of the function.

But humanity has taken a small step towards "better" from the meaning of "to live more good", and a big step towards its total knowledge. But, much of it is worthless, much of it is wrong:

1. The sense of honor, the dignity it develops so much so that it excessively seeks extreme dignity, which has no practical significance for

individuals or for all mankind.

2. Hereditary view, the concept of inheritance developed to one's descendants---. It actually refers to the "uncertainty" which have been defined of a "certainty".

3. The concept of "better existence" was, is depicted of enjoyments of material goods as being intoxicated and colorful, which induces people to open their eyes to everything until they obtain a Power for it.

This undermined quality of the key man, destroyed Sense of Mission Function, in general, socially. It undermines people's ability to judge "big issues, important thing".

To people, during thousands of years, small things was always right, big things was, are always wrong.

Worse than the consequences of indiscriminate selection randomly, why? The Sense of Mission Function was, is alienated, changed, there was, is only the worst choices.

Section 3:

Recognize Facts and Change the Status Quo

Scientifically knows social facts, it is closely related to the scientific improvement of society.

When the issue is set in the context of "human society", the Power of the state or the social system of the state which is (are) becomes a minor issue. If people's Sense of Mission Function be changed, human society could be a variation.

Restoring people's Sense of Mission Function which is not for the consideration of the realistic system or a Power, but for the consideration of human security and human direction.

Can imagine, complex Human Thinking Function is supposed to be preset, the basic human direction also conforms to the intentions of the Creator, but, think function was changed, the uncertainty and risks of human beings must be increased.

The Faith function and Sense of Mission Function have the greatest impact on the overall human beings and the overall direction of humanity. Among them, the Sense of Mission Function is more focused on the overall ability of the society.

At present, the common problems are the malformation of Sense of Mission Function and the malformation of the knowledge system. This situation is mainly caused by Private Power, but Public Power has not scientifically changed of the problems that have occurred:

1. The Sense of Mission Function Knowledge System have pointed out the "key points", it is extremely sparse, and its position is roughly on a state, ethnic groups, religious organizations and political parties.

2. The overall vitality of the society is monotonous.

3. Those who are willing to sacrifice oneself, sacrifice for Power, they are still regarded as heroes.

Wanted to change this situation, it is not about any specific dictatorial Power, because there are so many categories of dictatorial Power that there is no need to condemn them all or each one. And it's not about any kind of democratic power, because there are many kinds of democratic Power, some democratic Power is not good enough, they don't know what is called "civilized" what is called a "traditional" they are only intoxicated with the "civilization" "traditional", etc, they have become a model to be the failure of the human social system and be used as an excuse to dictatorial Powers. It makes no sense to condemn them now.

Theorem: the quality of Mission Function is directly related to the quality of Power.

The poor quality of power, must be to damage people's Mission Function, and were damaged people must be again to provide person for Power posts. If the Sense of Mission Function is not restored, both situations will continue.

Generally speaking, there are many social problems, there are countless social key projects, and it is the impossibility to rely on dictatorial power to accomplish them in a specified way, or any way. Democratic Power if lower the standards of "Person Content" start people freedom, it not enough to cover the countless "key points", even if that each "key point" have been free (uncontrolled) people filling in, without the Sense of Mission Function, not enough to bear the burden.

This is the scientific solution---to restore people's Sense of Mission Function. Let people take on their responsibilities. Let every key point of human society have people with strong Sense of Mission Function, display one's skill.

Chapter 8

Summary

A

There are two meanings in opening up new areas and acquiring new "known", try the application of Logical Function and Logical Rules using on new fields, the immediate meaning is to solve a numbers of specific problems.

The application of Logic Function and Logic Rules produced, produce something are the logical knowledge, which is convenient for inspection, convenient for inference even on a table, low experimental cost, and reduced trial risks.

The "known" listed in chapters 1 to 7 is suitable for applying Logical Rules in relevant matters. The basic principle is to analyze specific problems and specific matters to "known", and then find logical answers and solutions.

This is just the beginning, be fit for a random questions, a random topics for the relevant project.

For Social Science, you can try deep computing. Prepare for long-term planning, base on that find reasons from existing facts.

The calculation is that to deduce the mutual change relation of various social relations and factors, some static result in theory.---This must be complicated and difficult.

For example, a calculation of the "social factors" have several interactive relations, although was simplified is still difficulty, for example (and assumption):

1. The Person, are limited to four sub-items: four thinking functions.

2. The Unit of social activity is limited to one class, one sub-item.

3. The Power is limited to two sub-items: man and Unit of Social Activity.

4. The knowledge system is limited to three items already described.

Even so, the calculation of mutual change is more complex than the permutation and combination. It's need to take computer, it's need to take more people.

Above the calculation was a simpler hypothetical example, because that limited factors of interchangeability and the limited number of sub-items, the result is that: The results are simple, even meaningless or wrong. But this is science, and it doesn't have to hide anything.

As the understanding of the real situation deepens, the number of factors, items involved in the mutualism can increases to be closer to the real, the application value of the calculating results will be higher.

B

The important topic of this pamphlet is the Human Thinking Function.

Could be many ways, can try any one to describe the Human Thinking Function in order to get a more accurate and detailed for understanding of this fact.

The Human Thinking Function which obviously has more than four sub-items. Only four terms are used for deducting easily, was limited the precision standard which should be that limiting of the total number and types of conclusions.

This pamphlet does not draw many conclusions, but, a few conclusions may be all of them being on unwelcome, including the author himself, because it questions almost everything:

1. About human indicators, have put forward a new concept "Person Content", "Human Content", "Purity of Person".

Most people, myself included, are in a sub-healthy state and do not have enough "Person Content". --- No one likes such comments, including myself.

2. With regard to the Special Unit of Social Activity. ---An organization (institution) which was, is seeks power.

The most religious organizations and political organizations are unhappy.

3. Dictatorships, (Private Power, Enjoying Type Power) must be eliminated.

Dictators, beneficiaries of authoritarian theory, and so on are a huge camp, and they will not agree with this conclusion.---But the theorems and conclusions are all based on science.

4. Democratic institutions, (Democratic Power, Public Power, Responsible Type Power)--- Should be improved.

The objectivity of this conclusion need not be explained. Although people in a democracy may be unhappy, it seems acceptable. It should notice that the judgment which in basis of this conclusion it is the same as that of the previous conclusion, that is, the standard for examining the advantages and disadvantages of a Power or social system it is to check how treat about people or how treat about Human Thinking Function.

C

Social science is difficult in its early stages, and it is risky to study society objectively and scientifically.

It's as hard as you can imagine. The main reason is that the theory itself is not precision enough to know how long it will take for Social Science to become common sense. I don't know under what circumstances, the deepening research becomes fashionable.

Now, the risks or dangers are real to researchers for the following reasons:

1. Knowledge of making garbage or knowledge of making mistakes which be beneficial to the maker. It is, of course, dangerous to stand in the way of others.

This is a verifiable fact, and there are plenty of examples in society. It is useless to argue with these who create that knowledge and those who enjoy it. But this is only a theoretical risk.

2. Inferior Power makes ignorance for its living condition. The inferior quality of different grades they always are maintained by making different levels of ignorance. Therefore, all kinds of Power generally do not like to improve or change anything. Some Powers have created ignorance, such effects, have been that both aggrieve and the injured have been adapted to each other, and are associated with

each other.---These are not human being did---and, these are not Order-procedure did.

The real dangers of studying or promoting social science are as real as those faced natural scientists in the Middle Ages.

Finally, the question is, when you know all this, are you still willing to continue?

Postscript

I seem to feel that some political party organizations, religious organizations, think tanks and so on can be transformed into professional teams in the Social Sciences.

I am not sure that some groups have given up the pursuit of Power and can objectively study Power and provide objective thinking science.---Can human society have such a healthy religious organization or political party or professional scientific research institution?

But I am sure that human beings are the greatest creatures, else, anyone, that it only seems great briefly, they to obscures to the true greatness it is only extremely small and dirty.

One of the major problems for thousands of years, is that, human cooperation is not good enough, on the other hand, during collaborative process has generated the Special Social Activities Unit, then too many people to work for this Unit, until the social system for the Unit.

So, however, I assert that so long as people have determined to restore their thinking function, the degraded facts will be the past, success and great fruit are both inevitable outcomes because Creator and Nature are, is strong support(s) for this effort.

This world today is clearly a good place, a good time, with only about half of humanity's sense of mission function and belief functions alienated.

But on the other hand you can see one of the most dangerous moment has come, for the development of science and technology, the dictators and dictatorship in ignorance and ignorance of instinct, they are blindly incessantly trying to use the scientific method, to destroy human thinking function, to damage people's beliefs and sense of mission functions, if they succeed, human history will end, after that only is the world of the lower animals.

So I hope that every reader, everybody, has his or her own right decision to do something, even people who inside the Special Units of Social Activity who can wake up do something. --- That is Responsibility as a human being.

Thank you!

Fanzhu Meng.